Super Senses

Hearing

Mary Mackill

www.raintreepublishers.co.uk
Visit our website to find out more information about **Raintree** books.

To order:
☎ Phone 44 (0) 1865 888112
🖹 Send a fax to 44 (0) 1865 314091
💻 Visit the Raintree Bookshop at **www.raintreepublishers.co.uk** to browse our catalogue and order online.

First published in Great Britain by Raintree, Halley Court, Jordan Hill, Oxford OX2 8EJ, part of Harcourt Education.
Raintree is a registered trademark of Harcourt Education Ltd.

Editorial: Kate Bellamy
Design: Jo Hinton-Malivoire and bigtop
Illustrations: Darren Lingard
Picture Research: Hannah Taylor and Fiona Orbell
Production: Helen McCreath

Originated by Chroma Graphics (Overseas) Pte. Ltd
Printed and bound in China by
South China Printing Company

ISBN 1 406 20021 2 (hardback)
10 09 08 07 06
10 9 8 7 6 5 4 3 2 1

ISBN 1 406 20028 X (paperback)
11 10 09 08 07
10 9 8 7 6 5 4 3 2 1

British Library Cataloguing in Publication Data
Mackill, Mary
Hearing – (Super Senses)
612.8'5
A full catalogue record for this book is available from the British Library.

Acknowledgements
The publishers would like to thank the following for permission to reproduce photographs:
Alamy Images pp. **15**, **23a** (Inmagine), **7**, **23c** (Luca DiCecco); Corbis pp. **11l**, **22** (royalty free), **16** (Eye Ubiquitous; Robert & Linda Mostyn), **14**, **23b** (O'Brien Productions), **13** (Simon Marcus), **6** (Tom & Dee Ann McCarthy); Getty Images pp. **9** (Digital Vision), **4**, **11r**, **18** (Photodisc), **12** (Photographer's Choice), **17**, **19** (Stone); Harcourt Education Ltd pp. **5**, **10**, **20**, **21** (Tudor photography).

Cover photograph reproduced with permission of Harcourt Education Ltd/Tudor Photography.

Every effort has been made to contact copyright holders of any material reproduced in this book. Any omissions will be rectified in subsequent printings if notice is given to the publishers.

The paper used to print this book comes from sustainable resources.

Contents

Some words are shown in bold, **like this**. They are explained in the Glossary on page 23.

What are my senses?

You have five **senses**. They help you to see, hear, taste, smell, and touch things.

Pretend you are playing in a band.

What can you hear?

Hearing is one of our five senses.

What do I use to hear?

You use your ears to hear.

Sound comes into your ears.

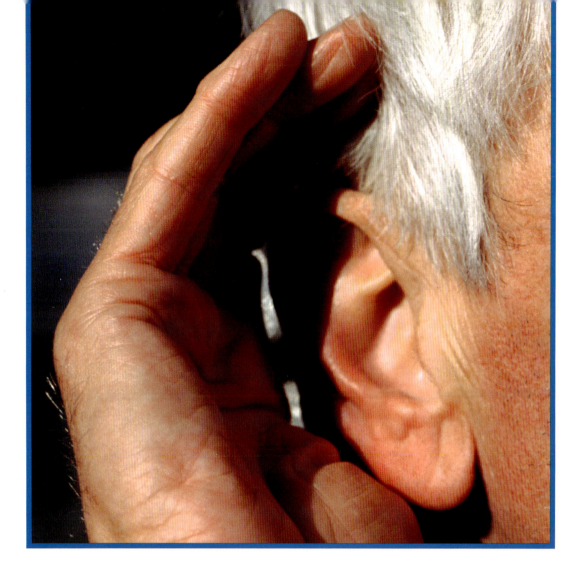

Your ears stick out from your head.

This helps them to pick up sounds all around you.

How do I hear?

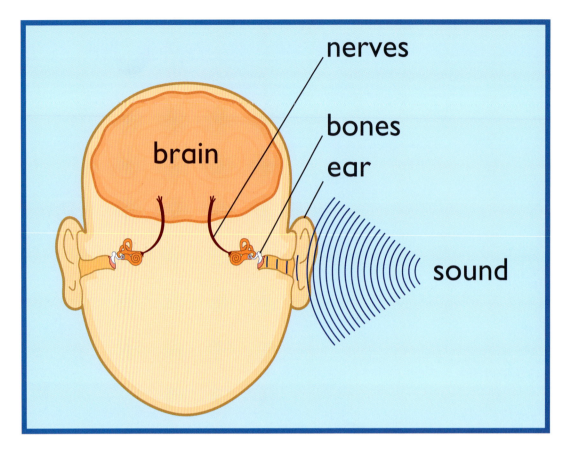

nerves

bones

ear

brain

sound

Sound hits some small **bones** in your ear.

Nerves send a message to your brain.

Your brain picks up the message.

Your brain would tell you that
these children are laughing.

What can I hear?

You can hear loud and quiet sounds.

lorry

birds

You can hear low and high sounds.

Which makes a high sound?

How does hearing help me?

Your **sense** of hearing helps you to stay safe.

You can hear cars or trains and get out of their way.

If you get lost, you can hear
someone calling you.

How can I hear things better?

A **microphone** can make people sound louder.

Headphones help you to hear music better.

They stop you hearing other sounds around you.

How can I look after my hearing?

Loud sounds can hurt your ears.

Cover your ears to protect them.

Try to keep your ears clean.

If your ears hurt, ask your doctor to look at them.

Animals can hear too!

Some animals can hear very well.

They can hear when danger
is near.

Some animals can hear sounds that we can not hear.

A dog can hear very high sounds.

Test your sense of hearing

Cover your friend's eyes.

Stand to one side and clap your hands.

Can your friend point to you?

You have two ears, one on each side of your head.

This means you can hear sounds from all around you.

Hearing is super!

Your **sense** of hearing:

- tells you how loud or quiet something is

- warns you if something is coming towards you

- means you can listen to your friends!

Glossary

 **bones** hard parts inside your body. The bones in your ear are small but very important for hearing.

 **headphones** something that covers your ears so that you can listen to music

 **microphone** something you speak into that makes the sound louder

 **nerves** parts inside your body. Nerves work with the brain to sense things.

 **sense** something that helps you to see, touch, taste, smell, and hear things around you

Index

Note to Parents and Teachers

Reading for information is an important part of a child's literacy development. Learning begins with a question about something. Help children think of themselves as investigators and researchers by encouraging their questions about the world around them. Each chapter in this book begins with a question. Read the question together. Look at the pictures. Talk about what you think the answer might be. Then read the text to find out if your predictions were correct. Think of other questions you could ask about the topic, and discuss where you might find the answers. Assist children in using the picture glossary and the index to practice new vocabulary and research skills.

Titles in the *Super Senses* series include:

Hardback   1 406 20020 4

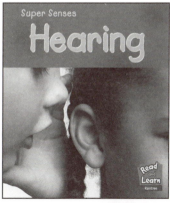

Hardback   1 406 20021 2

Hardback   1 406 20022 0

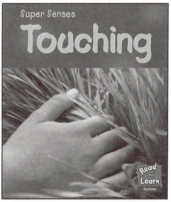

Hardback   1 406 20023 9

Hardback   1 406 20024 7

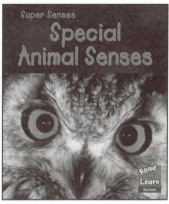

Hardback   1 406 20025 5

Find out about other titles from Raintree on our website www.raintreepublishers.co.uk